Dance

Ballet

By Trudy Becker

level 2 little blue readers

www.littlebluehousebooks.com

Little Blue House is distributed by North Star Editions:
sales@northstareditions.com | 888-417-0195

Produced for Little Blue House by Red Line Editorial.

Photographs ©: Shutterstock Images, cover, 7, 13, 24 (bottom left); iStockphoto, 4, 9, 10, 15, 16, 19, 21 (top), 21 (bottom), 22–23, 24 (top left), 24 (top right), 24 (bottom right)

Library of Congress Control Number: 2022919407

ISBN
978-1-64619-827-6 (hardcover)
978-1-64619-856-6 (paperback)
978-1-64619-911-2 (ebook pdf)
978-1-64619-885-6 (hosted ebook)

Printed in the United States of America
Mankato, MN
082023

About the Author

Trudy Becker lives in Minneapolis, Minnesota. She likes exploring new places and loves anything involving books.

Table of Contents

On Tiptoe

A girl stands on her tiptoes.

She moves lightly and leaps.

A boy jumps high in the air.
His arms and legs stretch out.

Another dancer
moves carefully.
She is graceful
and strong.
She is dancing ballet.

What Is Ballet?

Ballet is a kind of dance.

It started in France.

Dancers move skillfully with pretty shapes.

Dancers use positions. There are foot positions. There are arm positions too.

first position

second position

Dancers stand on pointe.
That means they stand on their toes.
It is hard, so dancers must be strong.

on pointe

mirror
bar

Learning How

Ballet dancers practice with
a bar and big mirrors.
They can see their moves.
Later, they dance on stage.

They wear tights on
their legs.
Some dancers wear tutus.
Tutus and tights help
show their moves.

tutu
tights

Dancers wear ballet slippers or pointe shoes. Pointe shoes help dancers stand on their toes.

ballet slipper

pointe shoe

Before showtime,
dancers stretch.
They put on their outfits
and go on stage.
It is time to dance ballet!

Glossary

pointe shoes

tights

positions

tutu

Index